Whereso

Whereso

❖

poems by
Karen Volkman

AMERICAN POETS CONTINUUM SERIES, NO. 155

BOA Editions, Ltd. ❖ Rochester, NY ❖ 2016

First Edition
16 17 18 19 7 6 5 4 3 2 1

For information about permission to reuse any material from this book
please contact The Permissions Company at www.permissionscompany.com
or e-mail permdude@eclipse.net.

Publications by BOA Editions, Ltd.—a not-for-profit corpo-
ration under section 501 (c) (3) of the United States Internal
Revenue Code—are made possible with funds from a vari-
ety of sources, including public funds from the Literature
Program of the National Endowment for the Arts; the New
York State Council on the Arts, a state agency; and the
County of Monroe, NY. Private funding sources include the
Lannan Foundation for support of the Lannan Translations
Selection Series; the Max and Marian Farash Charitable
Foundation; the Mary S. Mulligan Charitable Trust; the Rochester Area
Community Foundation; the Steeple-Jack Fund; the Ames-Amzalak
Memorial Trust in memory of Henry Ames, Semon Amzalak, and
Dan Amzalak; and contributions from many individuals nationwide.
See Colophon on page 108 for special individual acknowledgments.

ART WORKS.
arts.gov

State of the Arts

NYSCA

Cover Design: Sandy Knight
Cover Art: *Sundial* by Elizabeth King Durand
Interior Design and Composition: Richard Foerster
Manufacturing: Versa Press, Inc.
BOA Logo: Mirko

Library of Congress Cataloging-in-Publication Data

Names: Volkman, Karen, author.
Title: Whereso : poems / by Karen Volkman.
Description: First edition. | Rochester, NY : BOA Editions Ltd., 2016. | 2016
Identifiers: LCCN 2015050512 (print) | LCCN 2016001744 (ebook) | ISBN
  9781942683087 (paperback) | ISBN 9781942683094 (ebook)
Subjects: | BISAC: POETRY / American / General. | BODY, MIND & SPIRIT /
Dreams.
Classification: LCC PS3572.O3947 A6 2016 (print) | LCC PS3572.O3947 (ebook)
  DDC 811/.54—dc23
LC record available at http://lccn.loc.gov/2015050512

BOA Editions, Ltd.
250 North Goodman Street, Suite 306
Rochester, NY 14607
www.boaeditions.org
A. Poulin, Jr., Founder (1938–1996)

CONTENTS

One Might   9

What I've Come to Discuss   15
The City's Transparency   16
The Queen's Queen   18
A Walk in Calandrelli   19
All the A's   20
O,O   21
Beggar Rumination   27
Stranger Report   28
Rome Suite   30
Genova Superba   40

Have We Said Moments   45
As Noon Dawns   46
Memory Theatre   47
Cedar Spiking   48
O Thou   49
Three Dances   50
    Practice—gestures—tactics—resist
    Action Mechanics
    Rites of Spring
Nuit Blanche   53
Articulate House   56

Green Noise   63
Fatality Famed the Room   65
Iris Undulates   66
Canzone   67
Hellebore   69
Bridge   70
Three Films   72
    Drunken Angel
    Mr. Arkadin
    Giants & Toys

THE ROSY TONES   76
I WENT TO SIGN   78

VIABLES   81
ARCANA OF TROPES   82
WHETHER THE GOD   83
WHAT'S WRONG WITH THE HEAR   84
TEN WORDS   85
GHAZAL OF A LIFE   88
THE PASSAGE OF THE INTERVAL   90
PONTOON   91
I LIKE TO SEE IT LAP THE MILES   92
THE SPACES   94
SOLSTICE   95
GHAZAL OF THE DEAD   97
WHEN ONLY YOUR INITIALS ARE ENOUGH   99

Acknowledgments   *101*
About the Author   *103*
Colophon   *108*

❖

Whereso

ONE MIGHT

One might start here, with the blank specimen, not thinking too much or wanting to go home. Entrance is ample, the peak of the blank, a kind of acme in the ether. And what if you said No ceasing! No respite between night and pen. But it's not night yet, nor even crepuscular later, no haze blights the light, not yet, though the cycle progresses, you know it, contain it, know how it's measured in the movements of thought and body. Circadian authority, and also the way time breaks things, or is broken. Certain measurements portend that at such time in the morning . . . So many voices of requirement, regiment, the authority of this or that strident device, fetters that tap on the skin's head and need an answer. Why such indignation in violation, old friend? Who is addressed with these questions. Ghosts of persons. Sometimes the desire for contact can be a certain color, transparent or opaque, or clearly clear. Is clearness a color, or another form of smudge? Ocular weather is every kind, all times. Power dreams in its frame. In a pasture, boys lost in the wheat, the high grown weeds. By land or by water. O Athena, Medusa, pick up the phone! There are ropes and routes and other things to hold. Avert your eyes, sweet sisters, call in phenomena with the medium in hand. Apparatus, deuce of minus. Too much has been left to the tendency, the message, the flowers bursting and bowing on the verge, allowing all their semblance of edge to flash and measure. But a plot, we want a story, a root to grow and figure. Let's see, she's asleep, in a bed so big one mistakes it for a sea. Birds beat at the window, holy hibou and humble alouette. Stars and birds bide their colors, weave them in the tapestry that is desire's web at evening, a dark blue hearkening inundates the land. One approaches, bearing lantern. Is it the monster or Psyche? Is our sleeping sister really a sinner, or hermaphrodite hiding the secret sex she dies in? All quiet, all sweet, all needle-bright and bleeding. That was what we came to, that land, that stain, that blissful kindness of a liquid called forgetting. From its insides, distill a new sequence, a process that pleasures its

textures with a certain soothe. Or sooth, for we include bright
wisdom in the process, not the one of the foolish harridan, her
mouth a ruin, but that which springs from the thought's throat
like a sheer shade of begot. And all those things, those times of
the evening, collected in inkspots and nightbells, like a thread—
keep saying, I am doomed in the stains I shall remember, they
lay forgotten heads on the canopies, like a dress that spreads to
every corner of the stage. Ring down the curtain, cold auditor,
all is numen, an unctuous light activates the hand, and every
act loves the strange blue weight of its attending. So far, so
failing. What do we entail? A new contract or gambit, mask of
antiquity with all its spectrum of stare and frown. And grin, the
one hanging in the air like a lantern. Sometimes space needs a
sectioning, a kind of break in the turbulence of its hastening, le
vertige. Kiss the question, it's your longlost sweetheart come to
see you! I need a horse to escape, to bear me through the storm.
I don't like the story, the end is too heavy, a child plays near the
train tracks, make it stop! Some Russian catastrophe bearing
all away. Mine would be the black bread havocked at evening,
crude anchor of the norm. Five, six eggs in the basket, the hen
is ailing. Rain eats the roof. Night spies land. It was sailing like
a ship in a windy tinder, it lost its shore, now the black boat stays
on course, the trip will finish, and what you find won't be worse
than the event it was portending. What news of green? The stuff
of light and issue. We lost day somewhere, in the ambiguity of
twilight, smoke was solid in those heavy strikes, impermissible
flowers bled and bloomed in heaps around us. But this was no
grave, no petal or fragrant progress, it plumed its turn, a course
of nuance and shyness, we held the tips of our tongues, alive with
wonder! But shouldn't it be shrewder? Doesn't crude survival
dictate? The talking waters with their eventual hands. But no one
liked the weight, night's influx on the shoulders. Are we Atlas,
do the skies resist our unrestraining flesh? She knew so much
about bearing, the brightly borne. And are some things so light
they can't anchor on any shoulder? Hence the unbearable is the
levity that breaks and flies. No other woes but these, and the
sun goes. But she feeds all who need her, or makes a kind nest

for the vulture, with all her snows. Some nest, some frost, the place where the tongues rust. That wasn't a song, was a smite or incantation. As though war with the sun wouldn't break the darkest far. Roots bear, wind is rare in the forest of stasis. No more is a song mere breathing, smoke has shrouded any aptitude and cloud. Bird is a certain shade of whim, awake and inner. Network is the need's hurt, wounded, frail and spatial. Occasion, aureole. We return by runes, we know none free of symbols, we are a closed loop in the harm's heart, we don't forget. No leaps, no pipes, no happy forest gambol. Syrinx, you gave your bruised body for these sweets. As day never shed its many lights to be any person's present form. Sacrifice as a dream of freedom, but so is frame. No I can still or say it, bloodray, bright. Sometimes, some means, the eye grows weary, the fingers slur over keys, wounds, paper, the name of the topic was matter and all its ore. Or gold, or argent in the eyes' keep, saying never. Saying metal is precious which spills its ardent breath. Breathe but be not peaceful. Arcs decline in a curve, lovely and fatal. You are at every point, an actor, an archer, a specter spun and pensive. What night betrays you with its sentence, flight, thief, or barque of night traversing tarnished waters. So hum the spheres, alert with disappearance. So swells, dissembles. Core at the crux, indigenous, porous, as though green had a name for its tones, shapes, claims. A table will hold most anything you lay. A cup with its mouth saying fill me, faithful vessel. Are eyes just ruse, distorting every contact? Nothing helps, the mind is stained and will be its constant quotient of am-not. Rays rise and smite the outline, breeding flowers in the black benighted ground. So shall, so slow. A wheel is not an angle. Opaque erasures harmonize, where they absorb the frantic hammers, nothing will be like this light in its cloud of wild amber sifting, spreading. Sail, swirl, stall. Fearless candle, you are remedy and rule. This we knew, in our enfance, pale preliminary sounding. So far, so harm. Sometime there will be time, time less linear, more like the cloud with its clandestine take-me-hence. World implores, forebears, seeks its straying. There have to be these and those, swoops and frays. Colors there are no words for, opaque-clear, held in the eye like a stylus. Shine, inflection. So twines the name, soft fields of rumination, hard snows, bitumen littered in the loam. A coat, a wieldy blanket, some industry to glean. Leaf laws and freezes, summer of tabular data, where the blooming is doctored and discovered once and once. Bells, chimes, high buzz of fading flies, the city is called Aurora and you live there. You eat the flowers of its routes of leisure and cry Far. From this bench, at this moment the trees weep, bereft of season, the sermon you blur in your pocket is their mien.

WHAT I'VE COME TO DISCUSS

What I've come to discuss is mostly about shadows
and the airs left behind in caring, discarding,
the long inhibitions of whereso and when.
Alabaster, a dark quire, in its many pages and premises
the maze, from which move
tendrilled purples and contusions, magnificent
fuchsia receivers of false content,
the splayed flower, arterial, like the premise of a door
is where it leads to or from. Communication
of vessel, vial, capsule, hull, a tiniest nil
fires the neurons from their swooning stall,
is not a healing but adaptation to same
a quickening in deleting of sensation
a prior sizing. Stacked leaves (green shadows)
are givens in the columned garden, what work is needed
to determine that shape? Some hysteric
trope of repetition, rage for accretion,
dazed by its own mute replication,
like the minute lines of a hand. They are
its cries (writes Ponge, among others),
the tongue inseparable from its utterance (*langue*).
We weep to hear it, a language forgot.
I was saying I keep speaking
from some chamber sound deleted, which is why
I never call or write. In that theatre are many eclipses
and moons refracted in pinholes and wheels
wherein revolve astonished birds, and the Queen of Night
sleeps a rest restorative and profitable, and
andante allegro, the dead ships never sail.

THE CITY'S TRANSPARENCY

The city's transparency
gives way to its frames of animation,
the way names shape
expectation, a word's shift
tilts the plane.
                Water surges in the radiator
or it's just sound. The screen's blue wave
not a water mirror nor sky-scrim
nor eye-imprimatur
                      pigment-glint of plastic.
The yellow river, Arno or Neva, corrodes.
Ordering bridges whose other three sides
brace whole pulse,
                  space-wakeful
as a barely body
                paces its machine.
"I'm never sure/of after or before"
rhymes the child-mind
in its habit of eliding.

"Were the tree fir or poplar,
or the cottonwood topple/from its
eruption of mud" the real knowledge of real growth
in real material/enacts a sealing.

"Are they hearts, can they listen?" (in the phone).
An intonation like void-lights or someone
distributing seedlets to mechanical birds.
Nerves' inadequate dialect and the stammer
and the symptoms and occlusions
make it work.

"Do we scramble the figures/or constellations
of false stars?" Chart as might.

Chart charmed and startled
                with the rhythm of its design.
Some year to send tears and parings, already April.
To appear to self as flat roof
or wailing animal. Creator-creature in the box
it built and soiled.

THE QUEEN'S QUEEN

Or regality is the reigning
indemnity, this thread, as a silk strand
augments the meadow with its redness,
the dance proceeds, one clap, the sole stepper
a solarity, her "uncanny vulnerability"
as the player plays, the player's player,
Amphitrite. "A will of multiplicity,
an ocean," needs pageants and pomps
to entertain it, a mechanical dolphin,
a Tom called Arion, "spouting real water
from its blowhole, crown." I am merely
a carpenter, crafter
of magics, says someone, a secret
practice. But she
presses a whiteness to our eyes, a skin's
uncanny luminosity, "intrinsic
mobility of the element fire" as though fire
were cellular, and these vaulting
regenerations the royal
res. Her name is C or E, consonantal
vowel. Music the element
of fife or lute
or amplitude of the soundtrack
in historic playback. Depress the lever
of historicity, that story,
the lovelorn lover, hard duty,
betrayal. Her poisoned gown
of silk and semblance,
blooming mask, a player
of wonders, wedless.
She the projection of every season,
unchanging rain.

A WALK IN CALANDRELLI

A walk in Calandrelli park, branching allures: the gesturing statues, ornament or recipient or beckoning of bright past souls. The Roman copy industry's propagations, Greek imitations, automata of hours, paling with the years. That's a thin path leading past the hollyhocks to nowhere, and they're stacked, white-lilac, on a spine-slight stem, bent with their weight, in an afternoon's hot argent, words hang in this air, a heaviness caressing the leaves' green decorum, arching away from its shape, a tragic hammock. Whose humming threnody apportions this decay? Bird, what vernacular are you hurling? From inside the eater comes the swarm, from the strong flies sweetness. Honey of the carcass, and we swallow, tongue and worm.

ALL THE A'S

All the a's, the blurs, the we's, the articles indefinite, a specificity or stuttered plot. If you turn toward the green—the bole, the leaf, the stem—how it fuses the breezes whose transparent tongues are part of the bell's white notes and all they open. Were it noon—but it isn't, it's pallid meager one, we paint the sole peal on the hand's tender inner. Elsewhere the night is oppressing our distant kin, inversion that is radial and saturate and turns eyelids an actual amber, as the dark's wings demand that fragile canvas for its nest. And tears keep seeping, liquid, lucid, tongue-shaped, ornamental, in the mind-slipped interval, that silver suspension where you curl like a pebble in its raised and graven skull. Midnight's meticulous writing—few can read it, fewer view its reflection in dawn's sallow puddles or dew-lipped rivulets equivocating rue. Purple flower, cerulean wooing, clamorous fuchsia and alabaster spool, this floral machinery hums, sweeps, and dyes the pathways, in orient wheels of cambric and quick. Worlds bloom, and the light-flower, in bright-edged and windy minutes. Taint, hurt and shirring. A stemmed emendation. Or tide-light roaring. You are not my whom.

O,O

(Bare stage, seven dancers, white circle, black floor)

(Half are men, half women, the other either)

(Half wear white, the others black—they are dressed for
    suffering or leisure)

1:      I thought there was someone

2:   it sounded like someone

1/2:   someone close and pressing

3:   but I sense myself alone

4:      alone is an instinct

5:                                  gathered, compressing

6:      approximate weapon

7:      (as if to herself)   but I wasn't thinking

1 (smiling):   I love this place

2 (starting):   I wasn't there

3 (blinking):   How am I here?

4 (flinching):   I'm only waiting

5 (leaping):   but we like it, it starts with excess, it has a name

6 (grimacing): wears black and its lips are reddened

7 (hunching): as if in pain

1:     we tried not to go there

2:     shadows pulled under

3:     could sing it away

4:     (darting eyes in both directions) but continues

5:     what she feels . . .

6:     what you are feeling . . .

7:     (drops to her knees) and keeps starting

All: *as though in a circle—orbit or hell—*

1:     O my vocative

2:     o my polis

3:     o my om

4:     o ovoid, fecund and feral

5:     o oeil

6:     o my emoticon

7:     o oblate sum

(These two (pas de deux))

Their wills are plural

to rust, to sail

to nest and nautical

I didn't intend it

but anyway did it

it could be part of your worst dream, if you thought

but that she divided

thought from heart

(Next three) ("Déesse in flames")

I am stricken

graceless and this

torpor distinguishes

bad, it's hurting

it makes no sense

this shapeless moving

a kind of dying

it aches to learn

incapacity, shame

wasted motion

corrupts space but O

is all, absorbs and eats

and is open and empty

perfected

but what am I

(Last two) (low brood)

Did you or didn't you

ever occur

in such sumptuous spaces

empire founded in a scar

liberty, unqualified, entire

annunciation in an eye's aspire

bounding, beyonding

exile a mute returning

unending room

1:   Oh no

2:   uh oh

3:   o woe

All: *don't go*

4:   to flirt (she murmurs wryly) outside the circle

5:   to flout (he whispers wetly) the killing coil

All: *to look to foot to sport to howl*

     to spool to wheel to shy to toil

6:   it is part of our climate

7:   in the radius of seasons

1:   Orion's ozone

2:   or Orphic tone

3:   or zero-home

4:   an O, N.O.

5:   or ore, before

6:   shout-mouth, womb-bone

7:   around we go!

All: *to run in circumference, all edge, to know*

(They bow)

(Still in a circle, they turn their backs to each other, pause, then exit running to separate points off-stage)

(Lights down)

BEGGAR RUMINATION

Beggar rumination. Or think
"attenuated embers of famished fires"
replicating primed summers
empurpled with arson smoke.

Rewind. Re wind,
unfunneling its launch lines
inner gravure
neither void nor disclosure.

Exeunt, everyone.
Don't you hear the director?
Click your marks,
heels, hooves, halberds,

oscillations, oblate spheres.
If the stage quakes, just
relate it. Smite the
scene.

STRANGER REPORT

Agents don't look out the door or the port—are inner in their
traces and occasions—have sources of information and new
mediums—can contort. Their bodies are lighter and each fiber

forms a purpose. When it turns, it is powered from a center, sprung
from a source. As a light-source in a painting must diffuse from
one direction. We don't use real names—"real" and "names" are
terms and turns. The body's reality is a violence at play.

A thought-bubble might permit
new modalities of quiet
as a silent person's thinking resonates
multiplying space

as province, compartment, chamber, shard. Time (mute columbine)
where is your figured wheel in this betrayal? Immediate isn't in
it. And natural is a material (shroud or veil) and the tympanum
eats vibration, and the skull is a temple

where the priests are always ill. You are not a person but a
projection which moves. Echoes pervade the partitions and this
is presence (ghost, figure) along axes of possible motion

no gesture
can arrest
crawling or leaping
both are a deeping

of traceable action, intentions on a stage. We are your auditors,
calculating ruptures, in the invisible lines determining

movement as pattern, this precision beyond a norm.
Articulate body, a violent order, a stranger

rapport which finishes as stage and process.
Record.

ROME SUITE

Is opulence a fatality?
Polymorphic storm
in its echo of porous voice
What was it saying to the lines inside your eye
How did you trace them
in a light stark Roman
this time-slip fundament
booming acquittals
and the rest is rules

The scheme of the skull a repetition of form
Its sameness shakes us
Scheme: your blue head, its plausible dimensions
Strata: the norm which conforms it
I wanted the blue to make sense, be semblant
of the mind and its damaged children
Scheme: it keeps bleeding
in proper proportions
the space of this machine

Dioscuri, sun come down.

Sleep, burn. Birds burn in the sky's wheeled engine.

Emitted some pantheon's extension in each ken.
"Spherical as a dreaming orbit" "welt of form"
which streams the invention.

To plundered subjects, to plot our projects,
"a universal animation"
the capital of all this static beams its fact.

Capital, have you fathomed your extravagance?
An air's derangement of sequence, won't give.
Likely a goodly proximity to stateless.
Likely in ululation and expense.
My gasped expenditure is your wooden coffer.
My lungs reck the essence. They are sweet sacs
puffed with conundrum, a complex toxin.
Swains gad on the tarmac, are a-sky.

In the fruit of your hurt glows a helical

the dwarf (the nain) of introspection
in tears, again. You await
a levitation into clarity,
caressed decree, that one will love and suffer
in proper measure, hegemonic
calibration of the inner to cohere
with necessity, in its poise and noise,
an outer specter.

Materials, enclosure

shouting into the evening
that a god scar the soul in response
to be on the street, straying
to be a piece of ray, flame
when the sun's springs sweep the crossing
no one above or below, or out the window
no shadows to blight the projection
the project that is my name

Poor little piece of the baptism, the funeral
poor witness at the service
the flowers multiply, in brash bouquet
one should die under such mosaics
the tender sheep with their lightly lifting feet
the dome rings with their migration
to whom do you offer this devotion, shining lamb?
as you rotate the concavity
to arc, to stray
the stars in their holy fissures
shards of fires
the digits, the fingers
curled in blessings
and they rain
from the fist thrust through cloud
a totality of pieces
titanium is the will it worlds on
speaking frame

We dreamed in the impossible garden, stations blossomed.

Blossomed all in a single instant
like intensity's fruition a substance swelling
in transparent ether, an apex of clear.
Tilleul, panicle—corporeal verging.

We wanted the rapture to be tender, an awakening,
not this wall obliterating requital,
a stain on the actual, a dissident screen.
I keep it near: desolation, appraisal.
Keep it real, a god-hull in incidental fields.

Bird, impervious—bird, in brief arrest—

moment-states each and each
succeeding
a life collapsed into particles
which has its music too
sharp, perennial bell
a tone by instants forgotten
in the time of indeterminate collisions
what is a home?

That was my breaking
a moon's false premise
of shadow and disclose
kiss distilled into tubercle
aurora-stain of marble—
what do they mean,
the sable splayings, pink pilings, gesticulations
whose mind is the priceless
"database of intentions"?

Fermata: exit interior. exit imprecisely
Fermata: cats sleeping in the ruined foundation
Fermata: fraying thread of Ariadne
Fermata: the four rivers, the four clamors, the marble ardors
Fermata: forget what you came for
Fermata: pale church of x and o, San Carlino
Fermata: the ruined walls, the ruined statues, the ruined runes
Fermata: dust—dust-glitter—it was a building—it was there
Fermata: cardo maximus, the heart-road, the pulsing lex
Fermata: touch the vestige, the impressions, touch the when
Fermata: exit here. enter amplitude, roar
Fermata: forehead leaf-struck, a tiny greenness inscribes your
rest

More night than night, bat skimming the antiquity, it seems to
    be a puzzle
in stone-bright clay, a boundary converting proportion

to captivity, division. I was aways from here, a random wanton,
streaming white mesh like a net

and what was caught. Gray streaks, fulminates, shade on shade
a cascading throat, overflow

tipped to an inner, iris-clear. The owl's head with its 360°
rotation, your perspectives do dawn,

do orbit, shedding their spheres, hierarchies burst from their
    spirals
do coil. A seeing more than sight,

a saturation, as it ramps and turns—will apportioning the
    infinite,
what is this moment?—a nameless shaking,

it summons and takes.

The road brandishes a whip. Is a stern urger, seems to augur. Is my day-streak ribboned to a penance of heedless blue. Dawn of sleepless birds, in restless cypress. Sight exceeds, a grievous deeping, radiant iris, fume and fulgor, streams the pneuma from its stemless circulation, fluent web.

Tortoises burnish the fountain, above ephebes hoisting a marble concavity to heaven, feet impressing the head of a dolphin. Choreography of ornament, it completes its grace in the viewer's dazzled eye.

Degree, degree. This torn chord, that day. And we find it pitiless, the way it splits us, refits us. How a pulse is explosive interior, a ray ago. Shame, peccato. The figs' fate implicates the raven. A rat's nest, brown, hidden constellation. Elongates the vowel from its place of pure sound.

Dioscuri, the egg-born. Olympus to Hades on alternate days. Pageant, regiment. What was heard of the clouds' talk. A bearing, a verging, a mortal thorn.

Solstice

The night city becomes a day city
and is dirtier for it
the way light seems to plait
transparent tresses on these old airs
You think the cemetery is closed
where the tree falls, the remains
of this gray cadence where it states:
here he lies, dead of noise
the world's weight blankets
like this bed of daisies
fragrant in their sheathes

Sweet lights caress the Colosseum
o massive act
arches, perches
these windows precur
many-tongued Augur
as she enters
her mouths and shrouds
Are they hot, will they bite?
Will they arrogate plot to a shut surrender,
sleight of hand?
It could be wine splashing in the jugs,
a merry weaving. The lute, the pipe.
The lyre in its rational renewal—struck fret.

GENOVA SUPERBA

Med head—lozenges & drops—keep it talking
what's that pressure in the legs
descending from ears

"the sea's incoherences"
she says, but it was she
and not the sea

in the shell-skull
making waves
we weren't hearing. Si si, ok,

time's a waste, time's
a-wasting, and it's a matter of taste,
professor bluefish

why buy three when you can
get six, and watch them slit open
with the heads on

but mine
is full of zones
and omens, I don't think

you walk so fast
or it's more urban,
inventing banking

was inspiration
for the pesto,
correct?

Or an anchovy
looks me in the eye
saying stroke my spine

ticklish fish
bright funicular
swims out/in

I mind

HAVE WE SAID MOMENTS

Have we said moments are gods or questions?
It isn't worth thinking. Enunciatory your powers
bright tongue, I felt the air in its borderless containers
illuminate the sea, which through the shocked night
uttered its bodies. It keeps, keeps a blackness,
what do you say when you go, where are you going?
The room is a wandering on those turbulent depths,
sleep keeps swimming. It was more than a body I was
born in, it was a watery orchestration, water music,
should use a panoramic instrument, blood, chyle, salt,
is, should be, not tidal melody, more endocrine
(minutest ratio) of release, inhibition;
and sympathies with the blowing foam—
deity of a small propulsion of an instant's
ecstatic, explosive form (protean larme).
It will be another shine. It shall beguile.

AS NOON DAWNS

As noon dawns, dying the colors first gray, then umber, a blast
uncalling the garden, piece of hand, it leaves all its fellows
for a new kind of still. "Radial, wheels eat their spokes" and
it's a model, a sense you've forgotten or bled to its marrow.
"Teleology tomorrow unweaves," a mode of stridence, an
immanence blurring its tenses, will be, was. Thus grass-beds,
green and able, thus, then: a heliotropic sustenance looks up.
"I am looking at this white slip of silence, a shore's slight table"
in its remarking "tabulates the lashes" and pertains. How are
you calling, what are you burning? In what sentence have you
drowned your house, bright pulse? Who is the genius of this
window, in this shrill sail? A boat bites the sky, is no barque
cleaving cloud-waves toward the light. Is a following framed in
a fulgurance, starless smoke.

MEMORY THEATRE

Memory theatre. Things and words, in poised positions. Retrieved, they flood enunciation. An empty house, alive with secret sources—the scholar passes tapping his brow. "I left the idea beside this lintel" or "the imbrication lights the column" and twines it with silent ivies erupting skies. The speaker is spectator, shifting on the stage. She gazes on the bevels and boxes, each a singing planet. "My piano, my length of sail." The lion under the aspect will not eat.

CEDAR SPIKING

Cedar spiking to heaven, what can you say of green noon and its fertilities, its bronze delays, as the fountain apportions time with such transparent fissions, wet incisions—source stems. We were speaking of columns, sharp projecting lines, radiating from each thing shaken, as rays of roses make weep the scarred sun. Skin browns on the woman's bones, an affliction. "Projects from a soul's stain, outering" or is shade from a shadow falling— "throats, whelps, sharps, seeps"—an abstract pain, and eats its form. Wake me into fixity, a better dream than this pieceless collision. We were speaking of the links and the drops and the particulate borders, the pigments and chars. We were hectic degrees of declivities. We were burning.

O THOU

O *thou*, in a restless bracken, unbeseeching. It can be another hand. It can attain. I was looking behind each penumbra, a restless book. I was bent spine and pantheon of my own wet name. Thou in a slick upholding, thou afloat. Beatitude and stern Beatrice, awake, interred. It was nightless flying and a plenitude, incising. It was lung-sacs burst and avid, a voidless poise. Thou in a placeless premise, this celeste, and it seems to be motion, not ascension—seems it is a body unimploring, a human grain.

THREE DANCES

Practice—gestures—tactics—resist

Inflection: left sweep, humerus, arc, turn
Inflection: the dream's arm, the beat's wing
Motion: quarter turn, and seen

through the scrim, the seem-stain of its edging.
It is a field of gray-brown, a soft diffusing:
iris-rain. The bodies somber and phantom.

Some leg says, "Pulse and pause, arch, flex,
contract. This is kind of a step, kind of
sideways flying. This likes defying

space and what defines it." This like
defiance is a violence, primed set.
Thus like silence is a mime, a blind

beating at the border of variation.
Some hand says, "Come to the circle
of my grasp, soft task, dim slip

in my imprecision. I graze, I grip,
I pulse my fingers into scroll."
Turn to the turbulence of *from*—

core, medium, torso in its anchor,
its beyond. Torn air—accepts,
expels its entry, portal, key.

Then trails its shape, boreal, ghostly.
Part, turn. Deflection in a space, a twist:
the beat's swarm, the multiplying determine.

Inflect, deform.

Action Mechanics

A body only bounces a little—trajects in the impetus
leaves several infant motions in its going
Dodges steel and space, weights in the whir of
obstacle and no
barrier to launch, to cinch, to
curl in the pull, adduction
sprung—

a knee was dreaming
spatiality and then
a force that coursed

"nothing was hunting,
a joy that pushed me"

this leap to free

and lope to pole
gravitational shallow

"or sure there's more
measure to arrow"

in the impress of
a sighted sinew

assaulting wall

yes we bounce
it's a habit of survival

Rites of Spring

Forms—the woman whose chains are arms
who's hectic in her disparity
her tottered body.

They make a trajectory—
a partner, a wire—
a whirl into future

from the launch-point, fuse.
The dark down the chest
where the force fists—bruise.

Tense now—collarbone, column,
solid web.
The urge is sternum-stamen,

pollen flaming.
It shears the air,
scores the schism.

It persists.

NUIT BLANCHE

I.

Lots of times the statues are sitting over the questions.

The questions are flowers, in radiant shapes. Lovely the leaves of their sleeping.

A mouse crawls over the statue's bare breast. It climbs almost to the top, slips, drops.

This milky blue sky dreamed last night's *nuit blanche*, the moon bleeding silvery fumes.

The gold light through the iron tower was an exaltation of segmented space, unlike a choreographer wasting his dancers.

Or a dancer crying, My son has been arrested.

In shrill life we are mostly sleeping. The disruptions manipulate the leaves like speech is force.

A dancer resists force as gravity and bones' weight, launching sometimes into it, arc, jet. She inhabits a vast loudness, as the body is every language.

There is no need to shout. She shapes a more hideous anguish, flinching, writhing.

She is not Medusa. Don't destroy her.

II.

Augurs in atmospheres—speech more equivocal for those who don't control it. But not all lying is deliberate.

The body doesn't lie. Its cruelty is always true, its pleasure. It demarcates an atmosphere. It loves what language doesn't. It is an amalgam of edges, seeking their extension. It is a furious system.

Your speaking turns on baffled comprehension—phrases turned and repeated in English, Arabic, French—metaphor of translation and its failures.

It is too familiar—it dies in the air. Your dancers cower in their chairs, you forbid them motion. Abnegation of motion is a humbling, an expression of a mother's helplessness against abstract force.

She speaks English with a Spanish accent. She speaks French with the inflections of a Senegalese matron. You wish to make her many suffering mothers, in damaged speech.

But if war is violence done to bodies, why deny bodies the space to oppose it?

Bent spine of a dancer, her crown of dark hair.

III.

When you let her finally move, she desolates intention. Her limbs coil and twist, distorting muscle and form. We see and listen, a part of that pain.

Amplification exceeding the human—it shocks, deafens. Our bodies recoil from the shriekback, the screaming skirl.

Why make her faceless in her inhuman wail? Grief deforming the figure, a mother's hunger. Why make her a monster who shatters and voids?

Shock-shook, vibrations cave us. We can make no answer, hear no question. We escape to white night, the city's conversation.

Gold light, iron tower, exalting in the space it frames. The city enters our bodies, joins our noise.

The stage-cage lights up, empty. Dancers backstage can move now, can be a proof.

ARTICULATE HOUSE

I.

"I seek an articulate house, open
to sun and wind, perennial form
of a shell or hull protecting
the malleable," says Jane, "for I grow
fragile, in the seasons' wheel, and seek a window
which frames the earth and contains it."
"And light," says Janine, "and the means
to convey it, the eye ascending
in its pyramid of sight, builds its sane spaces,
its chambers of graces, consuming clouds,
and these are bodies." Dreams June, "arcs
and prisms . . . webs and seines . . . it is like
a glass but finer, it is a roof spun
nautilus-vial, a purling sail.
It is the membrane of an arrival."

II.

"Where is the safety of a paler day?"
says she, wan Jen, "for the terrible air
poisons the harbor, and the birds
will not come here. I remember
green ruminations, deflecting storms,
the tides in their stately shuttles, precessing
a passionate system, wise body,
chyle and sanguine circulation,
breathing frame." "Her aureate tones/
illuminate the ozones," rhymes Jin,
alert at dawn, uneasy watching
the colors of a tainting—stain the gray cliff,
"shale-black bones"—"but they are beautiful,"

whispers sifting Aurora, "fair, kind, true."
Jin twins "ecstasy and ague"—nothing new.

III.

Joan's house has bare concrete floors.
Walls, of foil-coated Sheetrock, are unpainted.
Her fixtures and furniture are metallic.
"I am sensitive to electromagnetic fields"
and the house feels her pulses, when she approaches
cuts the current, "inoculates electrodes,"
tracks her motions, encases her computer
in a metal-lined room. "The set projects
through a long metal funnel to the screen"
and the refrigerator, with a motion detector,
shuts off when she enters. "I need to live here,"
metal and desert, and the visitors bathe
with scentless soaps, then change into
clothes washed in special detergents, new initiates
to a sterile guardian temple, undefiled.

IV.

Allos—other. *Ergon*—work.
"It is a labor," says Jasmine, "of pointless
proportion." "Drifts everywhere and in,"
adds Jean, exhausted with structure—
invisible ardors, draining her stores.
"Fearful waking in predatory day,"
where there is no boundary. "Light collects
motes and toxins, and I am frightened."
"Night drains rumors of safety," murmurs
Juanita in the quivering whir.
"How can we live here?" these three cry,
stained land that blights intention,

"the earth a weapon, and the chemicals"
and radiant fields, the toils
puzzles of which one aids or ills.

V.

Three concrete sails arc into space.
They are two thousand years of exaltation.
Bright bows, leaping from a transparent box,
uniting rapture and reason. Their coating is
particle-eating titanium dioxide
maintaining its own pure equilibrium.
"I am my transforming spirit,
a windy building," says the strange ship,
"I touch my environment and change it"
cleansing the air which will kiss it.
"I am in that sense an act of being,"
a thinking material, changing its state.
"A blessing," muses Jess, as she reads it
online, "to gray ether and its bent attendants."
White ship, weird barque, sail on.

VI.

Julianna in the fields outside
the factory, two, three. Julianna
below the smoking towers, the porous
hours, the searing cores. The dirt steams
below her feet, "no ground beneath," this brume,
this boreas of mist, this turbid minus.
"There is something terrible in
reality," five, three, white shadow,
contagion in its muted din.
"Day again." Day and day. Dusk-dawn,
noon-column: smoke spills in diagonal

coils, never gone. Two drops puddle
on the glass, two are one. "Something
terrible and I don't know what." Yellow
despoils the guise. The skies unshut.

VII.

"I dreamed the bees stopped sipping the thyme-slips"
(this, Jill). "I dreamed silence, no shiver in
the lavender, no buzz. No fuzzed nubs
grazing the marigolds' ruffled buds."
"I dreamed birds dropped out of the sky,
in tens, in twos. See the beak? See the crushed
carnelian? Notice the look." "What answer
to their sweet questionings when
their element blanks, taints, kills them?"
"What can they ask with limp and twisted wings?
What syrinx thrills a shattered throat?" What note
in these bodies' admonition, bitter germ,
bitter worm of a bitter earth,
whose oblivious star scatters its spore.
"Bitter inheritance we breathe and are."

VIII.

"I seek an articulate house," says
Jaël, says Jade. Says solemn Judith
of turbulent hues. "I seek a home
in norm's affliction, where beauty
swells its ravaged sea—whorled foam
freaked with effluvium" and random
in its wrong genome: a mare
tenebrarum of ambient form. "Mundus
to mouth hard hurt, oculus to drift"
over the deformed animals of space.

"Where, then, is paradise?" Jamila broods.
"In the costumes of moods, moods' scrolling sleeves?"
Chorines with their consonance of scattered leaves
wresting a dignity from wides and waves
that array their wastings soundlessly, and stay.

GREEN NOISE

Oh you crazy baby.

Indemnify the vertebrae.

This strange shore of staying.

Isn't a form of motion, void

inscribed in the eyes, outcast

from your apostrophic dark.

They keep the luminous in further

zones of rooms, spatiality of the body.

Measures from, to. Are wrists

and writs, *pulsi* inscribing

the blood-bloom—surface foam.

Skin hum. I pressed my white hand

to the bunchgrass, it stung me.

There and then. A quittance, known.

Wind-scribbled cedar

enunciates the uproar, tidal,

perpetual. Ocean, mother

of numbers. Articulating

system—archaic vertebrae

or baby z.

FATALITY FAMED THE ROOM

Fatality famed the room with its double going.
It turned like sequence: set, set, portent,

like sea in the sky's fume, fumens et fumari.
I learned a little trick called me vince me.

Outside it was evening. Sky and its associates
continued singing. Storm never came.

We love the thunder with its voice,
loud hour, catalytic downpour,

opal-throat associates, vince bird.
Which actress was it played Athena

in the movie? Déesse of bright glances,
Athena Rossellini. She bears her robes

across the never-wetting waves, in the film
of shipwreck, straying, and final grace.

The myth of that system, fatality, turn,
like blood in the sea-spume, Clotho-vein,

red writ. The rétrouvé of the past-pulse, set—
Atropos Inexorable, bright slit.

IRIS UNDULATES

Iris undulates the lawn.
Burnt shell of aureole.
Sparrow skeleton hung from a skein.

I thought it was part of my story, the thousand I's.
Robin song from the chimney, couldn't see it.
Coxcomb redbreast, dimmer vaunting.

I sure was happy to find you
skinny and reddish, like a red pine
unconscious of its redness, it is so tender.
There are stars and blurs where the words were.
They keep nesting.

I sure was unclouded by your clouds
though they kept westing, blackening
the valley with their splays and shrouds.

Not sure the green z of my eyes,
gold a, swept the gray-blue of your ocular
lake-scrawl spill around the pupil.

Lumen rifts around aurora's room,
sifting. This isn't the sad song
songing. This be a swift space deleting

where we drift.

CANZONE

Diffusion into lamplight—the suspect will
blunts its tongues on the night's green propulsion,
a tangent same in its ardencies will
argue the sameness of dark and its will
to conception, to flame's extinguishing
of will, the phantom branchings,
willing endings. The night
clothes itself in glass. So
close to a vertical motion, this
will to succession, a mind of glass.
Do the glassy minutes spill
their seconds, like curves of a spiral

or glassy spool,
revolution of will
that skirls in a radius
precessing the spool's
compulsion to uncoil?
The black glass night created to spoil.
The shale of its outside, its skin
of reception. It caresses
the concept, a prettiness,
compact. The spills
close, and their seep
leaves a trail, a stain close

to putrefaction, a rotted clothes.
Spinal in a vertebral
consequence, disclosed
as a rejection of closure
makes of will a mirror,
far or close
to the open its infant clothes
shivers into pulsions.

It is spring's compulsion
to close sweet snows
in nights of winter concept,
blooming warm dawns of reception,

a brown glass the blood receives
like petals unclose
in a sun's mind's conceiving.

This is the name a dirt is receiving,
a fresh spill awakening.
Dead on reception, we gleam,
a dark perceiving.
Isn't will a glass
that saturates its willing?
Or perceives its own perception?
A compulsion to believe
the body's compulsion

lives beyond propulsion,
past mereness of receiving
attraction, revulsion,
like a dumb bug, convulsing
a world closed in glass.
The lamp pulses its coil
of distance and suspension.
The heart-spool won't stop.
Is a spiral, embodied motion.
The pulse urges, red completion,
propitiation of will.
It sounds, a willful

accretion, that will
not be silenced by repletion.
Crimes of reception
can never kill or close
the glass pierce of their spiral.

HELLEBORE

She says, The range of this tone will reach an apex, somewhere
along the wall, which blocks its circle. The motion tends to the
perpetual.

Or, she continues, a furthering of purpose. The day or night
comes first? asks the sophist. Must we establish a noun, to couch
a tendence. Parting the clouds of etymology, testing the boundary
of a chambered sky.

Of stars and scars. World-animals, ensouled beings.
"Something like living
beside a mountain's bald slope,
incapable of knowing
the proud pines and vernal pool
beyond the sight's arc."

And yes we have seen it, intractable, stoic. And the tender
wildflowers that nest there, calling to the tips of fingers, "Caress
me with hesitancy, a frail degree."

And "the lake that was the valley" a form of only. It taints the
sleep—pellicle, ripples—veining the dead
in the railroad graveyard, charnel ground,

corporeal speech, a seeking that leaves.

BRIDGE

1.

Bridge's absence gave the creek a new aspect.
Uncrossable, irascible. Crosser stems
on the bank with her will and form,
extension. "Phantom of incapacity
which is me." Bright roar of water,
x of indomitability.

2.

The bridge is not an x. It bridges nothing.
The turmoil is only a portion.

3.

Bridge on the grass is brideless.
Tufts of terra like a bloom in air.
Rational slats, a surface's accretion,
slat system. Grass tints it, heliotropic
emanation, sharp, up, or complex
occupation in shiving rain.

4.

Creek's uncrossability, a new beauty.
"It looked like the process of a thinking,
deep run." It became the suffering of form
and mute suggestion. The syllables
were not perennial. They broke and grew.

5.

The blue pants of the crosser were neither sky
nor water. They orient to the body
as form and boundary. The crosser's green shirt
neither grass nor leaf-thought.
Desire to not get wet, another hurt.

6.

"Glamour of limit, where the rocks just slant"
down the bank, in a wet

stratification, and the creek
spills blows and goings
and is omniform leaving, a prime of seem.

7.

High water as a contour of relation
swells, hurls. The creek which was other
but not antipodal, or refusal. "The wish
to touch it with my phenomenal hand"
loves it as material.

8.

The bridge made the force containable.
Bridgeless the crosser sits, and very still.
"My phenomenal body crosses and longs."
Ceaseless body of the audible.

THREE FILMS

Drunken Angel

The swamp simmers, the guitar blurs.
Typhus in all of us. Or tuberculosis
means holes in the lungs

for gangsters and gamines
and will alone
can kill it, the bacilli

gathering forces like teeming
infestations, pure war. Night
a gray haze slurring over

fevered Tokyo—yakuza
plucking flowers, dodging slippers
the mistress throws,

and the doctor swigs alcohol
tinged with tea, but in the end
bears gently the four

shining eggs for his dying
friend. Cure is an integer
of desire for life, honor,

and the code broken
means dying in white paint,
spat blood, slick and slipping,

almost swimming, or drowning
as in a white marsh
unstable footing, the lung collapsing

and spat blood in black & white
a dim tone, spectral seeping,
the dying grimace finally

a pain-code, a frame.

Mr. Arkadin

Mr. A. buries his past in the long noir corridors of postwar
Europe, some violent work in Tiflis, '27, Sophie's gang in
Warsaw till the pretty dancing girls put her out of business, the
200 K Swiss dollars burning holes which she says were pure
gold and stolen, when Guy finally finds her in Mexico married
to the general, the sun blurring strange in the bw, the white
cities gray-toned and the heat a speculative season, what was
crazy in love what was conundrum, the gamine daughter an
implausible cause for the litter of bodies on two continents,
buying a telescope, feeding the fleas, poor Zuk never gets his
goose liver (with potatoes and apples), poor Guy don't get the
girl though she's beautiful, because you're my friend I'll give
you something, this name, dying beneath the vast crate chalked
Milano, poor Milly can't remember the Russian, the masquerade,
the number of years on the tombstones, empty plane circling,
the beard doesn't scare because it's ridiculous, the money does.

Giants & Toys

Industry loves me. Its gooey sweets and gap-toothed kisses.
Send the invoice to a profit named Delicious.
Aren't you tired of samurai and gardens?
The black test car is a lodestar.
The girl looks like Anna Karina with cherry shoes.
She laughs at the ballplayers, their waggle
of bats. The bubble-helmet of the spacesuit,
spent projection, the outfit has a human
dimension, as humans occupy a cosmos
or social body. Anthropometry of economy,
made of tongues and anuses, sumptuous
matrices, penetration and disgrace.
Lover, you are some fast car, or sugared water.
You look like you're from Tokyo or Long Island.
Same, am.

THE ROSY TONES

"the rosy tones
stroking the ozones"

such sights
ocular requitals
space entails

and oh but it's gray
but the gray is neutral, soothing
to the thing that is wrong

in my syncope, body
out of song with its boundary
hey sleepy but it isn't

a good wake, a dream sand
a drowning in
fantasms/forms

the kiss of space
sweet sequence
but weight

in the night
pressing the breath down—
Morpheus

in your procession
of darker voicing
voce tenebrae

beautiful room
empty
weight stains

the song

I WENT TO SIGN

I went to sign my name on the sky's back. I raked grain from its swaying vertebrae. Bright stem. I am eating everything it makes me, in the imprimatur of letter—my name a crop and raging. It said, Fair signatory, on your murmurous mount, do you give so much of gray grievance as fits a rock's mouth, a raw rock gaping its chambers? What color is the sun there? Why is its spine so broken? Vertebral fingers, a personal tool. Its scale is your state and facet. It is sustaining.

VIABLES

Viables! The small plate is large. The class starts too early.
The beautiful day turns ugly. Black ice. Some creature
climbs the tree, scuttle of claws and fur-frieze,
trunk blanking its snout. No apple core, no slimed
cilantro, will rot that pile. No late wintry, sleepy easing,
few birds returning.

Spectrally speaking, the sun wounds and downs, spikes its
    setting,
fangs the eyes. I hoist a book between me and it.
It dazzles around it. It, it, inharmonious house,
the it-hit no intimate you can protect through.
Curve a curtain why don't you. Hit-run.

Pay attention. A too-wit, a to-who, sere words, mere
letters. Weird mirrors. More airs. A creature clambers,
its face erasing. A disgrace. Plank of pages displacing
a house in space.

ARCANA OF TROPES

Arcana of tropes
beguiled as a muse would say
chance it or
don't. Ecstatic?
Euphonic? To think only
fortune sees double, servile
goggle staring out its puny
hide, spore-core
interior, intimation or blame.
Just, heck, hermetic.
Kabbalah,
listing its privates,
misting its pivots, dreaming
names. Not norms nor
orbits: obits.
Prosthetics. Soul is a
question? (Quotation.) Can it be
replaced? More's the pity, none's the
symptom, lies the sign.
Touched quite, torchon and
undulation, something forms.
Volumes. Volutes.
Whelks—unlovely shell.
Xerxes reports scourged seas.
Your ire, Alexander, your information,
zero sums.

WHETHER THE GOD

Whether the god is flawed or fraud
or the ocean understands its cruel miracles
or the hand of the maker forms as calyx or canker
framing the hazy scaffolds, the spectral billows.
You think "cat"—fur and flicker,
hunch and saunter—you think "evasion,"
a survival notion, a fog, a phase.
A creature devours its interior. It seeks an exit.
Swarm of marvels to delete it. Game of days.
See the paradigm? It isn't shifting. It spits and hits.
I cross out the name you gave me, never mine,
simulated body of smoke and neutrinos.
I slit the dress down the back to break myself out.
See it there on the chair beside its twin,
the one that you cut.

WHAT'S WRONG WITH THE HEAR

What's wrong with the hear, Doctor?
It feel weird. It don't hear
or like a brick block
it egress to wind
full of sounds and rondures—
noise bends the microscopic
hairs random directions and they sing
a false alarm, coded wrong—
dumb codice, shrieking
your dead falsetto
castrati nerves
shrilling to no purpose.
The cortisol
full-throttle
swells the endocrine,
prolapsis of a functioning system
and I sense a clear space
(clear song, clean line)
in this hive of misperception,
is it mine? Been wrong
so long, been down
and awkwardly footing
these wild and whirling words.
Swear ghost, dissonant receiver
of dirty pulsings
you'll bless my vengeance
(my tables) on these wiles.
I read it, I dreamt it, I was it,
mute and buzzing—
iconic static—
white poison dripping in.

TEN WORDS

Alcohol

Bombay Sapphire, jewel-bottle blue.

Also wines, the grape varietals I do not know.

Noise

"Life's nonsense pierces us with strange relation."

In Missoula, muted hum of cars on I-90.

Loud-throated magpies.

Deer scattering in the bracken: a system.

What's all the bellowing about—you'll frighten the fish!
The men on the bank fall silent.

Postcard

I often buy postcards when traveling, or take the free ones, intending to send them to this or that person. But I never send them. I am always muted by the small square of space—so small and white—by the extremity of saying something so brief—by the ungainliness of my handwriting, magnified by the spareness of the frame. I have many stacks of postcards in my desk, from many trips, all blank on the back, which this or that person will never know was meant for them.

Civilization

Flood waters—median strips—wheelchairs—rats.

Depression

When not depressed: the American Depression Industry, with its pills, books, experts, tinctures, talking cures.

When depressed: saturate, leaden blackness in skull and chest.

Study

Brown study, gray study—fugue, absorption. I study languages for their raucous dispositions, constellation of intelligent sounds.

Worries

Inquietude, unquiet, disquiet.

A word is a worry. And never sorry.

Newspapers

I let only a few in the house each week. They quickly grow from thin sheets to massed blocks, and it is almost impossible to remove them. A few months ago, after much effort, I carried some blocks to the garage—an intervening step to putting them on the street for collection. Now the garage is full of newsprint blocks. Some have begun to tilt or slip from the top—making them less implacable, but more menacing, capable of impetus, momentum, mutations in form.

Reading the news online, an occasional spasm grips the screen, as the latest update is imprinted. This violent amendment has its own mode of disquiet, but its proliferation, immaterial, stays thankfully out of sight.

Medicine

My insomniac pills. The first, Donormyl, came from a pharmacy in Paris. A tiny white cylinder of 3o pills cost 3o francs, while a small pack of Nurofen (ibuprofen) was a staggering sum. I tried other European pills—the homeopathic Dolisedal (requiring three doses under the tongue, at specified intervals before and during sleeptime)—the frightening Stilnox from a pharmacy in Spain (warning of possible impact on the central nervous system). Now Temazepam is my nightly potion, Ambien for extreme occasions. I've read of a next generation of pills, from a lab in Japan: Lunesta, beautiful, pseudo-Latinate name.

Do these drugged sleeps tint my dreams, my wakings? Dark stain behind the eyes which never sees.

Simplicity

Nullity. A word and never sorry.

GHAZAL OF A LIFE

Click, clock, as you nibble the time of a life.
Yawn, years, as you swallow the prime of a life.

What's that noise—time's wingèd chariot? Bruiting birds?
Abrasive racket, this chong and chime of a life.

The old house needs a new deck. Closet doors dismember.
Will Death, the final mortgage bill, be next, the dark subprime
    of a life?

Rugosa shoots pink between the thorns.
Apricot bows with frail fruit—the brief sublime of a life.

Aphids swarm the spongy pepper, slugs suck the buds.
Too fecund yard, too fertile forms, muck-mired grime of a life.

How to spice this heaving stew? A fresh leaf, a fragrant umbel?
The usual suspects—parsley, sage, rosemary, and thyme of a
    life.

Paupered, plundered, pirated, pillaged—sacked, looted,
    mobbed, daubed, Job'd.
Left just one song, a perennial "Brother can you spare me a
    dime" of a life.

Even dreams crack with disaster—drowned cars, malevolent
    crowds, bleeding eyes.
This teeming grind, 24/7 overtime of a life.

Running on karma—did a past self chop heads?
Who can account for even one ruin—that unsolved mystery,
    the crime of a life.

What light glares up ahead? Police interrogation? Divine
 beyond?
Terrestrial tinsel, that glow—glitter-ball, strobe or lime of a
 life.

And that gambler with the razzled hair and weedy eye—
watch her place her bets on this scheming rhyme of a life.

THE PASSAGE OF THE INTERVAL

The passage of the interval of the occasion
the prolapse of the item of the inclusion
the matter of the effect of the unknown reason
begging leave, the analytic's a poor persuasion
the sophist and the gymnast in misprision
the sartor, spectre, the temblor trahaison
unbecoming in a manner of my position
unrespecting the romance, the geranium prison
microscopic mire, blinkered magnification
Argus and Cyclops eternally arguing the squint division
of a world of shreds, shards, and shrapnels, rents and torsion
pugilist views, split enigmas, a rhyme a dozen
as in the impetus of the arc of a wave unhidden
sees, sings, a siren.

PONTOON

Pontoon in the pitch of the current's crimped position.
Pontoon in the motorboat's wake, scuds the winks.
Pontoon aftless, portless, stolid, unsailed.
The water, luminous onyx, volcanic rock.
The water with its rifts and sticks, its limned detritus.
A few clouds, in skiffing whiteness, a few white sounds.
And the sky in its canvas flatness, a blue contrivance.
And the trees in their serried rows of green, in their
verdurous blur, relentless repetition, green hum.
And the curvature of the mountains, the rondure soothing,
    static, inhuman.
Only the water is a solid, but mutable, collapsing, gelling.
The scrolls, the tulles, the chisel-splits—knolls, notches, nodes.
The bell, the lull, the supple rill, the sudden
union into stippled pattern, then a muting, a deforming, a
    dissipation.
On the boat, they eat, they talk. Mostly they watch.
Mostly they feel the ferocity, the order, the artless, acheless
    element
holding them up.

I LIKE TO SEE IT LAP THE MILES

I like to see it lap the miles.

I like the derangement of roads, their lines, their minus, their sequestered edges, their bordering crops. Their traversing of a highway's numbering, sequence, flow.

I've been too long in my crate, says the cat.

I like the slim meanders, the numbing rumors. Normal, Fargo, Fosyth, somewhere to go. The plot portends, the map laps. I like it: rest stop, N. Dakota, arc-en-ciel. Floodless promise, painted canyon, a liking.

●

Ripped fabric of the box springs, an interior cats hide in.
I upend.
Two cats slide out, fur gimcracks.
I can't explain.
Distance, interminable sunder, this room.
A purring interiority, that car.

●

It laps. My two feet feed it, my arms extend its contours. My shoulders hold. I extend its outline, its bounding form. I norm it. It enormes me. It corms my mind, I'm mostly engine. I'm drive, blind schism. I don't touch land. I'm touched by. Endless sunset, W. Minnesota. Fines double in zones. Zones define. Distance, skying.

●

Let me out, says the cat. Outside, an exit.
We're "in" the car, metal shell, vague shelter.
My carapace, or tremulous extensor, or dinged career.
This windshield, segmenting landscape, with a rippling crack.
Long crack, charting an episode, cardiographic, seismic.

You should get that fixed, said my sister.
I didn't. Its eloquence—bell-curve, brandished—its jagged
    swell.
It hurts to look.

●

The cats sleep, a third night. It hurts. Turbulence, a roar shirring
windows. Susurrus, hum.
Inner ear eats elevation. Body, motion, mountain, this rise we're
riding, a "gain." Walking is alien, the body's weight the wrong
tension. The wrong burden. Not my freight, say the feet.
It caught me sleeping.

●

Mountain: valley: sign: name.
Beyond liking, the lapping, impersonal, opaque.
The lack of a limit in spite of numbers: miles, gallons, dollars.
We "lose" two hours. We go back in time. We're very west and
    north. The air is drier.
Extensor. Strange career. Fourth animal. Only home.
Bounding outline that laps and saps. Hard hide.
We like it.

THE SPACES

The spaces of the loved house enlarge
after absence, the reds of the red pots
engorge their iridescence, the bright breaks
the road-whelmed eyes, the body tremulous
with miles, the shudder in the car-core,
the bones' interior, the ceiling higher, the traffic
quaver. The rooms boom. Body smaller, older,
unfamiliar, a fragile filter, a thin vibrating string,
struck sum. Is it home? This echoing resonance,
high tomb. This calculus, unlikely correspondence,
rung dome. The body drowns in its bounty,
hums in its staunch solidity, its syntax,
its sun-smote windows, lucent alchemy, the process.
Laurel in the pot. Rosemary for remembrance.
The body will blur its boundary, will embrace.

SOLSTICE

Amniotic light
bleeds through the blinds,
ceding a hush, transposing
dawn to an
ether, an ore
finessed, unfinished, under-
gone. An effort
Herculean or
Icarean? Wings, fists.
Just jeweled japes, maybe,
koine for
liminal states. For
murmuring margins,
narcosis, dowsing
obfuscations. Not
penitent, not perfected,
quirked into clarity, a
rhythmic
solidity seeking
terminus. Will it
unveil
veracity, voraciousness, the
wake? The morning, the insinuating
exit, the vaulting
yonder, the dimming
ziggurat, the where.

Zampini, little feet,
you feint a restlessness, remorseless.
Exigency tapping on the
window—what's below?
Vermilion, viridian, all
unctuous colors,
tapers obscuring

solitary stations. This
reduction—call it
quickening—this fame,
predestination,
orison—this
nomenclature resumed. Some
mnemonic. Some animal,
lustral, sleek, a sounding bell.
Known. Will it call
juniper, jasmine, junco
irradiating names? Will it
hail the air with particulars?
Gems, germs, gestures.
Fevered care. It
emerges into elegance, from
dream. As
calamity, as
brilliant birth, blighted.
Actual, impersonal, through.

GHAZAL OF THE DEAD

Then I think we are only the spawn of the dead.
Kitten, tadpole, larva, puppy, cub or fawn of the dead.

Post-winter, spring clambers from the brown.
The quickened dandelion, a yellow-eyed espion of the dead.

"Chrysanthemum growers/you are the slaves/of
    chrysanthemums," wrote wise Buson.
Shin-deep in bindweed, yanking, cursing, I'm the sweaty pawn
    of the dead.

In zombie movies, they're so buxom, burly, tearing live meat.
Audiences thrill at the muscle, heft, and brawn of the dead.

No effete tormented vampires. No youth grown pale and
    spectre-thin.
Steven S., dead of AIDS at 26, first showed me *Dawn of the
Dead*.

"Trim the antennae, sharp tip, jagged rostrum, legs and feet."
"Suck the orangey brains," reads the recipe for lime-marinated
    prawn of the dead.

The deceased eat the living, the living chaw on them.
Cannibal culture—devour first or be quartered and drawn by
    the dead.

That night at Steven's was a double feature.
First lurching zombies, then shrieking Texans, the about-to-be
    chain-sawn of the dead.

Demon barbers, *Soylent Green*, *Delicatessen*? Tantalus, Titus?
Let's grok long pig. Irresistible, that spicy saucisson of the dead.

Vegans have their reasons. So do condors and crows.
Most days, I'd rather gnaw on than be gnawn by the dead.

In the historic Missoula graveyard, tombstones familiar from
    streetnames—Higgins, Arthur, Brooks.
The peaceful grounds, mowers humming, like a bowling green
    or lawn of the dead.

Mid-June, beautiful day for a father's quadruple bypass.
The sky, lustrous, sleek, like a grandiloquent yawn of the dead.

Winter will wander back, leaving its scabs. Just bluff and laugh.
Lie in bed New Year's Eve watching *Shaun of the Dead*.

"Christ, the original airplane"—Apollinaire. Great spirit, lusty
    poet,
drink wine, eat wafer from that high avion of the dead.

And you Volk, with your deeps and slumps, your wine-dark
    lees,
who will you feed when you join the hungry gone of the dead?

WHEN ONLY YOUR INITIALS ARE ENOUGH

If outside is the new inside, "smoke and mirrors
translated into clothes," the textures and tinctures

of these silks, these folds and glowings—
simulacrum as emanation, tone, name—

sleepy, like a sweep of cloaks, dreaming
of torsos in the empty white boutique.

Or "austere but anatomically implausible
designs" grafted from the mannequins

in deformed chains, " a determined
abstraction of nature and life,"

life's mnemotechnical abstraction,
nature's mechanical propulsion.

Dear monk, I love your cloak.
One day my life was a cowl

without a hem. "Voluminous trousers
with deep crumb-catcher cuffs"

an implausible rebuff. But it seemed
as much of paradise as we could speech.

Fruits of the body, inaudible as roots.
Fabric's temerity, the pin wit bit.

I thought and thought, but nothing came out.
Weeds grew from the plot. I tear and wear them.

ACKNOWLEDGMENTS

Thanks to the editors of the following journals in which some of these poems first appeared: *Black Warrior Review*, *CutBank*, *Denver Quarterly*, *New American Writing*, *1913*, *A Public Space*, *Purple Journal*, *Octopus*.

"One Might" was published as a limited edition letterpress chapbook by The Press Gang, Brooklyn/Tuscaloosa, 2008. Thanks to Christina Baik. It was also included in *American Poets in the 21ˢᵗ Century: The New Poetics* (Wesleyan, 2007), edited by Claudia Rankine and Lisa Sewell.

"The Queen's Queen" was inspired by Cate Blanchett's performance in *Elizabeth*. Additional references are drawn from Stephen Greenblatt's *Will in the World*, Francis Yates' *Giordano Bruno and the Hermetic Tradition*, and the DVD special features.

"O,O" owes its initial inspiration to Deborah Hay's collaborative dance "O,O," performed by seven dancers at the Centre Pompidou as part of the *Festival d'Automne à Paris*, 2006.

"Stranger Report" is a response to Richard Siegel's multimedia performance "Stranger/Stranger Report" at the Théâtre National de Chaillot as part of the *Festival d'Automne à Paris*, 2006.

"Memory Theatre" draws on the description of the Memory Theatre of Giulio Camillo in Francis Yates' *The Art of Memory*.

Three Dances: "Practice—gestures—tactics—resist" is after the Paul Taylor Dance Company, "Action Mechanics" after Elizabeth Streb, "Rites of Spring" after Elizabeth Streb.

"Nuit Blanche" responds to William Forsyth's dance/performance piece "Three Atmospheric Studies" performed at the Théâtre National de Chaillot as part of the *Festival d'Automne à Paris*, 2006.

"Articulate House"—Section III adapts language from the *New York Times* article, "In One Arizona Community, an Oasis in a Toxic World" by Fred A. Bernstein, July 10, 2005. Section V was suggested by the *Times* piece "Church on the Edge of Rome Offers a Solution to Smog" by Elisabetta Povoledo, November 28, 2006. Section VI is drawn from Michaelangelo Antonioni's *Red Desert*. Much of the initial impulse for the poem came from that film and from Todd Haynes' *Safe*.

Three Films: *Drunken Angel* by Akira Kurosawa, *Mr. Arkadin* by Orson Welles, *Giants & Toys* by Yasuzo Masumura.

"I went to sign my name on the sky's back" was commissioned for the exhibit *Manual Labors* at The Belmar Lab, Denver, Colorado. Thanks to Jake Adam York for inviting me to participate.

"What's Wrong with the Hear" is for the French doctor who tried to cure my tinnitus.

"Ten Words" was an assignment by Elein Fleiss for the bilingual *Purple Journal*—the words are in the alphabetical order of their French originals.

"Ghazal of the Dead" quotes Buson from *The Essential Haiku*, translated by Robert Hass. The prawn recipe is from Andrea Nguyen's *Into the Vietnamese Kitchen: Treasured Foodways, Modern Flavors*.

"When Only Your Initials Are Enough"—the quoted phrases are from the *New York Times* article "In Milan, All Masculinity, No Pretense" by Guy Trebay, July 26, 2008.

My thanks to the Bogliasco Foundation for a generous residency during which some of these poems were written. Thanks, too, to the American Academy in Rome for a Visiting Artist Residency, and to the University of Montana's Office of International Programs, President's Excellence Fund, and College of Arts & Sciences for funding to support it.

ABOUT THE AUTHOR

Karen Volkman is the author of *Crash's Law*, *Spar*, and *Nomina*, and a chapbook, *One Might*. Her work has appeared in over 3o anthologies, including *American Poets in the 21ˢᵗ Century: The New Poetics*, *The Pushcart Prize Anthology*, and *The Norton Introduction to Poetry*. Recipient of awards from the National Endowment for the Arts, the Academy of American Poets, the Poetry Society of America, and the Bogliasco Foundation, she teaches in the creative writing program at the University of Montana in Missoula.

BOA EDITIONS, LTD.
AMERICAN POETS CONTINUUM SERIES

No. 1   *The Fuhrer Bunker: A Cycle*
         of Poems in Progress
         W. D. Snodgrass

No. 2   *She*
         M. L. Rosenthal

No. 3   *Living With Distance*
         Ralph J. Mills, Jr.

No. 4   *Not Just Any Death*
         Michael Waters

No. 5   *That Was Then: New and*
         Selected Poems
         Isabella Gardner

No. 6   *Things That Happen Where*
         There Aren't Any People
         William Stafford

No. 7   *The Bridge of Change: Poems*
         1974–1980
         John Logan

No. 8   *Signatures*
         Joseph Stroud

No. 9   *People Live Here: Selected*
         Poems 1949–1983
         Louis Simpson

No. 10   *Yin*
         Carolyn Kizer

No. 11   *Duhamel: Ideas of Order in*
         Little Canada
         Bill Tremblay

No. 12   *Seeing It Was So*
         Anthony Piccione

No. 13   *Hyam Plutzik: The Collected*
         Poems

No. 14   *Good Woman: Poems and a*
         Memoir 1969–1980
         Lucille Clifton

No. 15   *Next: New Poems*
         Lucille Clifton

No. 16   *Roxa: Voices of the Culver*
         Family
         William B. Patrick

No. 17   *John Logan: The Collected*
         Poems

No. 18   *Isabella Gardner: The*
         Collected Poems

No. 19   *The Sunken Lightship*
         Peter Makuck

No. 20   *The City in Which I Love You*
         Li-Young Lee

No. 21   *Quilting: Poems 1987–1990*
         Lucille Clifton

No. 22   *John Logan: The Collected*
         Fiction

No. 23   *Shenandoah and Other Verse*
         Plays
         Delmore Schwartz

No. 24   *Nobody Lives on Arthur*
         Godfrey Boulevard
         Gerald Costanzo

No. 25   *The Book of Names: New and*
         Selected Poems
         Barton Sutter

No. 26   *Each in His Season*
         W. D. Snodgrass

No. 27   *Wordworks: Poems Selected*
         and New
         Richard Kostelanetz

No. 28   *What We Carry*
         Dorianne Laux

No. 29   *Red Suitcase*
         Naomi Shihab Nye

No. 30   *Song*
         Brigit Pegeen Kelly

No. 31   *The Fuehrer Bunker:*
         The Complete Cycle
         W. D. Snodgrass

No. 32   *For the Kingdom*
         Anthony Piccione

No. 33   *The Quicken Tree*
         Bill Knott

No. 34   *These Upraised Hands*
         William B. Patrick

No. 35   *Crazy Horse in Stillness*
         William Heyen

No. 36 *Quick, Now, Always*
        Mark Irwin
No. 37 *I Have Tasted the Apple*
        Mary Crow
No. 38 *The Terrible Stories*
        Lucille Clifton
No. 39 *The Heat of Arrivals*
        Ray Gonzalez
No. 40 *Jimmy & Rita*
        Kim Addonizio
No. 41 *Green Ash, Red Maple, Black
        Gum*
        Michael Waters
No. 42 *Against Distance*
        Peter Makuck
No. 43 *The Night Path*
        Laurie Kutchins
No. 44 *Radiography*
        Bruce Bond
No. 45 *At My Ease: Uncollected Poems
        of the Fifties and Sixties*
        David Ignatow
No. 46 *Trillium*
        Richard Foerster
No. 47 *Fuel*
        Naomi Shihab Nye
No. 48 *Gratitude*
        Sam Hamill
No. 49 *Diana, Charles, & the Queen*
        William Heyen
No. 50 *Plus Shipping*
        Bob Hicok
No. 51 *Cabato Sentora*
        Ray Gonzalez
No. 52 *We Didn't Come Here for This*
        William B. Patrick
No. 53 *The Vandals*
        Alan Michael Parker
No. 54 *To Get Here*
        Wendy Mnookin
No. 55 *Living Is What I Wanted:
        Last Poems*
        David Ignatow
No. 56 *Dusty Angel*
        Michael Blumenthal
No. 57 *The Tiger Iris*
        Joan Swift

No. 58 *White City*
        Mark Irwin
No. 59 *Laugh at the End of the World:
        Collected Comic Poems
        1969–1999*
        Bill Knott
No. 60 *Blessing the Boats: New and
        Selected Poems: 1988–2000*
        Lucille Clifton
No. 61 *Tell Me*
        Kim Addonizio
No. 62 *Smoke*
        Dorianne Laux
No. 63 *Parthenopi: New and
        Selected Poems*
        Michael Waters
No. 64 *Rancho Notorious*
        Richard Garcia
No. 65 *Jam*
        Joe-Anne McLaughlin
No. 66 *A. Poulin, Jr. Selected Poems*
        Edited, with an
        Introduction by Michael
        Waters
No. 67 *Small Gods of Grief*
        Laure-Anne Bosselaar
No. 68 *Book of My Nights*
        Li-Young Lee
No. 69 *Tulip Farms and Leper
        Colonies*
        Charles Harper Webb
No. 70 *Double Going*
        Richard Foerster
No. 71 *What He Took*
        Wendy Mnookin
No. 72 *The Hawk Temple at Tierra
        Grande*
        Ray Gonzalez
No. 73 *Mules of Love*
        Ellen Bass
No. 74 *The Guests at the Gate*
        Anthony Piccione
No. 75 *Dumb Luck*
        Sam Hamill
No. 76 *Love Song with Motor Vehicles*
        Alan Michael Parker
No. 77 *Life Watch*
        Willis Barnstone

No. 78   The Owner of the House: New
         Collected Poems 1940–2001
         Louis Simpson

No. 79   Is
         Wayne Dodd

No. 80   Late
         Cecilia Woloch

No. 81   Precipitates
         Debra Kang Dean

No. 82   The Orchard
         Brigit Pegeen Kelly

No. 83   Bright Hunger
         Mark Irwin

No. 84   Desire Lines: New and
         Selected Poems
         Lola Haskins

No. 85   Curious Conduct
         Jeanne Marie Beaumont

No. 86   Mercy
         Lucille Clifton

No. 87   Model Homes
         Wayne Koestenbaum

No. 88   Farewell to the Starlight in
         Whiskey
         Barton Sutter

No. 89   Angels for the Burning
         David Mura

No. 90   The Rooster's Wife
         Russell Edson

No. 91   American Children
         Jim Simmerman

No. 92   Postcards from the Interior
         Wyn Cooper

No. 93   You & Yours
         Naomi Shihab Nye

No. 94   Consideration of the Guitar:
         New and Selected Poems
         1986–2005
         Ray Gonzalez

No. 95   Off-Season in the Promised
         Land
         Peter Makuck

No. 96   The Hoopoe's Crown
         Jacqueline Osherow

No. 97   Not for Specialists:
         New and Selected Poems
         W. D. Snodgrass

No. 98   Splendor
         Steve Kronen

No. 99   Woman Crossing a Field
         Deena Linett

No. 100 The Burning of Troy
         Richard Foerster

No. 101 Darling Vulgarity
         Michael Waters

No. 102 The Persistence of Objects
         Richard Garcia

No. 103 Slope of the Child Everlasting
         Laurie Kutchins

No. 104 Broken Hallelujahs
         Sean Thomas Dougherty

No. 105 Peeping Tom's Cabin:
         Comic Verse 1928–2008
         X. J. Kennedy

No. 106 Disclamor
         G.C. Waldrep

No. 107 Encouragement for a Man
         Falling to His Death
         Christopher Kennedy

No. 108 Sleeping with Houdini
         Nin Andrews

No. 109 Nomina
         Karen Volkman

No. 110 The Fortieth Day
         Kazim Ali

No. 111 Elephants & Butterflies
         Alan Michael Parker

No. 112 Voices
         Lucille Clifton

No. 113 The Moon Makes Its Own Plea
         Wendy Mnookin

No. 114 The Heaven-Sent Leaf
         Katy Lederer

No. 115 Struggling Times
         Louis Simpson

No. 116 And
         Michael Blumenthal

No. 117 Carpathia
         Cecilia Woloch

No. 118 Seasons of Lotus, Seasons of
         Bone
         Matthew Shenoda

No. 119 Sharp Stars
         Sharon Bryan

No. 120 *Cool Auditor*
Ray Gonzalez
No. 121 *Long Lens: New and Selected Poems*
Peter Makuck
No. 122 *Chaos Is the New Calm*
Wyn Cooper
No. 123 *Diwata*
Barbara Jane Reyes
No. 124 *Burning of the Three Fires*
Jeanne Marie Beaumont
No. 125 *Sasha Sings the Laundry on the Line*
Sean Thomas Dougherty
No. 126 *Your Father on the Train of Ghosts*
G.C. Waldrep and John Gallaher
No. 127 *Ennui Prophet*
Christopher Kennedy
No. 128 *Transfer*
Naomi Shihab Nye
No. 129 *Gospel Night*
Michael Waters
No. 130 *The Hands of Strangers: Poems from the Nursing Home*
Janice N. Harrington
No. 131 *Kingdom Animalia*
Aracelis Girmay
No. 132 *True Faith*
Ira Sadoff
No. 133 *The Reindeer Camps and Other Poems*
Barton Sutter
No. 134 *The Collected Poems of Lucille Clifton: 1965–2010*
No. 135 *To Keep Love Blurry*
Craig Morgan Teicher
No. 136 *Theophobia*
Bruce Beasley
No. 137 *Refuge*
Adrie Kusserow
No. 138 *The Book of Goodbyes*
Jillian Weise
No. 139 *Birth Marks*
Jim Daniels
No. 140 *No Need of Sympathy*
Fleda Brown

No. 141 *There's a Box in the Garage You Can Beat with a Stick*
Michael Teig
No. 142 *The Keys to the Jail*
Keetje Kuipers
No. 143 *All You Ask for Is Longing: New and Selected Poems 1994–2014*
Sean Thomas Dougherty
No. 144 *Copia*
Erika Meitner
No. 145 *The Chair: Prose Poems*
Richard Garcia
No. 146 *In a Landscape*
John Gallaher
No. 147 *Fanny Says*
Nickole Brown
No. 148 *Why God Is a Woman*
Nin Andrews
No. 149 *Testament*
G.C. Waldrep
No. 150 *I'm No Longer Troubled by the Extravagance*
Rick Bursky
No. 151 *Antidote for Night*
Marsha de la O
No. 152 *Beautiful Wall*
Ray Gonzalez
No. 153 *the black maria*
Aracelis Girmay
No. 154 *Celestial Joyride*
Michael Waters
No. 155 *Whereso*
Karen Volkman

COLOPHON

BOA Editions, Ltd., a not-for-profit publisher of poetry and other literary works, fosters readership and appreciation of contemporary literature. By identifying, cultivating, and publishing both new and established poets and selecting authors of unique literary talent, BOA brings high-quality literature to the public. Support for this effort comes from the sale of its publications, grant funding, and private donations.

The publication of this book is made possible, in part, by the special support of the following individuals:

Anonymous x 3
Nin Andrews
Angela Bonazinga & Catherine Lewis
Nickole Brown & Jessica Jacobs
Bernadette Catalana
Christopher & DeAnna Cebula
Gwen & Gary Conners
Anne C. Coon & Craig J. Zicari
Gouvernet Arts Fund
Michael Hall, *in memory of Lorna Hall*
Grant Holcomb
Christopher Kennedy & Mi Ditmar
X. J. & Dorothy M. Kennedy
Keetje Kuipers & Sarah Fritsch,
in memory of JoAnn Wood Graham
Jack & Gail Langerak
Daniel M. Meyers, *in honor of James Shepard Skiff*
Boo Poulin
Deborah Ronnen & Sherman Levey
Steven O. Russell & Phyllis Rifkin-Russell
Sue S. Stewart, *in memory of Stephen L. Raymond*
Lynda & George Waldrep
Michael Waters & Mihaela Moscaliuc
Michael & Patricia Wilder
❖